ALL-TIME FUNNIEST JOKES

ABOUT ANIMALS

Little Mitchie
an imprint of Mitchell Lane

Creating Young Nonfiction Readers

Little Mitchie lets children delve into nonfiction at young reading levels. Young readers are introduced to new concepts, facts, ideas, and vocabulary.

Tips for Reading Nonfiction with Young Readers

Talk about Nonfiction

Begin by explaining that nonfiction books give us information that is true. The book will be organized around a specific topic or idea, and we may learn new facts through reading.

Look at the Parts

Most nonfiction books have helpful features. Our *Little Mitchie* titles include color photographs and graphic aids, a table of contents, a glossary, and an index. Share the purpose of these features with your reader.

Color Photos and Graphic Aids

A lot of information can be found by "reading" photos, charts, maps, and other graphic aids found within nonfiction texts. Help your reader learn more about the different ways information can be displayed.

Table of Contents

Located at the front of the book, this list shows the big ideas within the text and the page numbers where they can be found.

Glossary

Located at the back of the book, the glossary defines key words and phrases that are related to the topic. These words and phrases can be found in the text in colored type.

Index

Located at the back of the book, an index is an alphabetical list of topics and the page numbers where they can be found.

With a little help and guidance about reading nonfiction, you can feel good about introducing a young reader to the world of *Little Mitchie* nonfiction books.

Mitchell Lane
PUBLISHERS

2001 SW 31st Avenue
Hallandale, FL 33009
www.mitchelllanepub.com

Little Mitchie

First Edition, 2025.

Author: Kim Thompson
Designer: Kathy Walsh
Editor: Luana Mitten

Names/credits: Kim Thompson
Title: All-Time Funniest Jokes
About Animals / Compiled by Kim Thompson
Description: Hallandale, FL:
Mitchell Lane Publishers, [2025]

Series: All-Time Funniest Jokes
Library bound ISBN: 979-8-89260-262-4
Paperback ISBN: 979-8-89260-421-5
eBook ISBN: 979-8-89260-273-0

Little Mitchie is an imprint of
Mitchell Lane Publishers

PHOTO CREDITS
Shutterstock: Alyson W. Kast, cover, 1; V_ctoria, cover, 1, 22, 23; Phai, 4, 16, 18, 20; @DoyanDesign, 3, 4, 6, 8, 10, 12, 14, 16, 18, 20; eli eliyev, 4; DniproDD, 8, 14, 16, 18, 20; Valery Kachaev, 4, 8; Luthfi Ikhsan, 4, 6; Katya, 5, 7, 11, 15; Lori Sparkia, 4; Gert Kotze, 4; Randy Rimland, 5; Cory Thoman, 5; Marina Popova, 6; millenks, 6; Dora Zett, 7; Susan B Sheldon, 7; smutan, 8; Bildagentur Zoonar GmbH, 8; Eric Isselee, 9; Vivid Pixels, 9; Johan Schoeman, 10; Shanvood, 10; Viorel Sima, 11; Ermolaev Alexander, 11; Nadzin, 12; Mumut, 12; HappyPictures, 12; Sararoom Design, 13; GoodStudio, 13; Russain, 13; Nestor Rivera, 14; Sergej Razvodovskij, 14; stockphoto mania, 15; Clara Bastian, 15; Susan Flashman, 16; Harry Collins Photography, 16; Nynke van Holten, 17; Ken Benner, 17; klyaksun, 18; Jessica Guarnido Guerrero, 18; Artur Aliev, 18; xyxx, 19; Suzanne Tucker, 19; Zuzana Gabrielova, 20; Yupa Watchanakit, 21; Buch and Bee, 21

CONTENTS

AT THE ZOO

Q: WHAT ANIMAL IS OUT OF BOUNDS?
A: AN EXHAUSTED KANGAROO!
Q: WHAT ANIMAL CAN PUT PEOPLE TO SLEEP?
A: A HYPNO-POTAMUS!

Q: WHAT DO YOU CALL AN AARDVARK WHO PLAYS UNO?
A: A CARDVARK!

Q: WHY ARE LIONS SUCH TERRIBLE STORYTELLERS?
A: BECAUSE THEY ONLY HAVE ONE TAIL!

IN THE FOREST

Q: WHAT DO YOU CALL A WOLF WHO USES BAD LANGUAGE?

?!

A: A SWEARWOLF!

Q: WHY SHOULD YOU ALWAYS LISTEN TO PORCUPINES?

A: BECAUSE THEY HAVE A LOT OF GOOD POINTS!

IN THE NEST

Q: WHAT DO SICK BIRDS NEED?

A: TWEETMENT!

Q: WHERE DO OWLS SHOP?

A: AT THE OWLET MALL!

Q: WHAT DO BIRDS DO FOR FUN?
A: THEY PLAY FLA-BINGO!
Q: WHEN DOES A TEACHER NEED BIRDSEED?
A: AT A PARROT-TEACHER CONFERENCE!

AT HOME

Q: WHAT IS A CAT'S FAVORITE NURSERY RHYME?
A: THREE BLIND MICE!

Q: WHERE DO DOGS NEVER SHOP?
A: AT THE FLEA MARKET!

Q: WHAT PET DOES A MAGICIAN HAVE?
A: A LABRACADABRADOR!

Q: WHAT DO CATS GET FOR A TREAT?
A: MICE CREAM!

IN THE OCEAN

Q: WHO TOOK THE BABY OCTOPUS AND HELD IT FOR *RANSOM*?
A: SQUID-NAPPERS!
Q: WHAT DOES A SHARK SAY WHEN SOMETHING IS GREAT?
A: "JAW-SOME!"

Q: WHAT DO WHALES EAT FOR A SNACK?
A: SHIPS AND SALSA!
Q: HOW DID THE DOLPHIN GET TO THE HOSPITAL?
A: IN A CLAM-BULANCE!

ON THE FARM

Q: HOW DO YOU FIT MORE PIGS ON A FARM?
A: YOU BUILD A *STY-SCRAPER!*
Q: WHAT DID THE NANNY GOAT SAY TO HER KID?
A: "IT'S *PASTURE* BEDTIME!"

Q: WHAT IS A CHICKEN'S FAVORITE TREAT?
A: A COOP-CAKE!

Q: WHERE DO YOUNG COWS GO AT LUNCHTIME?
A: TO THE CALF-ETERIA!

IN THE JUNGLE

Q: WHAT SNAKE LOVES DESSERTS?
A: THE PIE-THON!
Q: WHAT TIME IS IT WHEN 10 ELEPHANTS ARE CHASING YOU?
A: TEN AFTER ONE!

ON SIX LEGS

Q: WHO RULES THE INSECT WORLD?
A: THE MONARCH BUTTERFLY!
Q: WHAT HAPPENS TO BEDBUGS IN LOVE?
A: THEY GET MARRIED IN THE SPRING!

Q: WHICH BUGS WEIGH LESS EVERY YEAR?
A: LIGHTENING BUGS!

Q: HOW DOES A FLEA GET FROM ONE DOG TO ANOTHER?
A: IT ITCH-HIKES!

BY THE POND

Q: WHAT TIME DO DUCKS WAKE UP?
A: AT THE QUACK OF DAWN!
Q: WHERE DO TURTLES GO DURING AN EMERGENCY?
A: TO A SHELL-TER!

Q: WHAT DO FROGS ORDER WITH THEIR BURGERS?
A: FRENCH FLIES!
Q: WHY DOES A FISH ALWAYS KNOW ITS WEIGHT?
A: BECAUSE IT HAS ITS OWN SCALES!

MORE LAUGHS

What could happen after it rains cats and dogs? *You might step in a poodle!*

What is more amazing than a talking owl? *A spelling bee!*

What alligator wears a vest? *An investigator!*

Why don't crabs share? *Because they're shellfish!*

What animal loves snacks the most? *A chipmunk!*

Why do cows make good acrobats? *Because they're so flexi-bull!*

HOW TO TELL A JOKE

1. Relax. If you feel awkward, your audience will too.

2. Don't rush. Give your joke some space and trust that it's a good one!

3. Vary your tone. Your voice should not be flat or boring.

4. Pause right before the punchline. This will add some drama!

5. End right after the punchline. Don't keep talking or try to explain.

6. If you don't get a laugh, that's okay. Try another joke!

GLOSSARY

"I GET IT NOW!"

aardvark (AHRD-vahrk): an African animal with a long sticky tongue that it uses to catch insects

exhausted (ig-ZAWS-tid): very tired; worn out

pasture (PAS-chur): land where animals can graze on grass

ransom (RAN-suhm): money demanded in exchange for someone who has been kidnapped

sloth (slawth): a tropical mammal that has claws, long arms and legs, moves very slowly, and hangs upside-down in trees

sty (stye): a pen or enclosed area where pigs live on a farm

INDEX

FURTHER READING

Cheeky Monkey. *Hilarious Jokes*, Puns, Riddles & Pranks: *A Tickle-Your-Funny-Bone Book for Silly Kids Who Love to LOL*. Atglen, PA: Better Day Books, 2024.

Katz, Alan. *The Funniest Joke Book Ever for Kids!* New York: Scholastic, 2024.

Riddleland. *The Jumbo Book of Funny Jokes for Kids*. Prospect Park, PA: BCBM Holdings, 2023.

ON THE INTERNET

Good Housekeeping: 125 Knock Knock Jokes for Kids and Adults Who Love to Laugh https://www.goodhousekeeping.com/life/parenting/g36198919/knock-knock-jokes-for-kids/ Silly jokes to fool your family members and friends!

Parents: 100 Jokes for Kids That Will Actually Make You Laugh https://www.parents.com/fun/entertainment/14-jokes-for-kids-that-will-actually-make-you-laugh/ A source for Dad jokes, one-liners, puns, and more.

Today: 150 Funny Jokes That Will Get the Family Laughing https://www.today.com/parents/family/jokes-for-kids-rcna49138hat/Find jokes about seasons, animals, and more.

ABOUT THE JOKESTER

Kim Thompson is a teacher, writer, and editor. Things that make her laugh out loud include going down waterslides while holding her feet in the air, trying to balance a grape on her nose, and the dopey expressions that turtles get on their faces. She lives with her husband and two funny cats in Columbus, Ohio.